Praise for the poetry of
Alan Walowitz

Alan Walowitz's poetry can take a dream, memory or reflection, take a snapshot or present an image painted with his use of language, bring the reader into the moment, and evoke thought and emotion.

~ Peter V. Dugan, Nassau County (NY) Poet Laureate, 2017-19

It was W. C. Williams who said, "If it ain't a pleasure, it ain't a poem." So, Alan Walowitz's poems are full of pleasures, laughing out loud ones, heart-wrenching ones and wise ones, some that took my breath away.

~ Colette Inez, author of *The Luba Poems*

What I love about Alan Walowitz's poems—a genre that I call Alancholy—is the very relatable way in which he captures so many of life's important moments with astute observation, wry humor, and empathy. He has a distinctive voice which infiltrates my synapses and resonates with my heart.

~ Betsy Mars, author of *Alinea*

Alan Walowitz is neither withholding nor unnecessarily oblique. And then there's the welcome wit, as he juggles the sometimes Jewish-blues in deft narratives that never cease to surprise, Walowitz is unafraid to write, 'We've known these people from the ache of having lived.' In his refusal to claim wisdom, he is wise. And oh, so rare to turn a breath into a gasp.

~ Estha Weiner, author of *at the last minute*

Alan Walowitz's poetry can provoke out-loud laughter and pensive melancholy; better still, he can even do both in the same poem. You find yourself thinking about a Walowitz poem even after you've read it twice and put it down. He has a particular talent for reconstructing recollections, quietly showing us what is moving about them and why, as in this volume's splendid title poem.

~ Robert Wexelblatt, author of *The Posthumous Papers of Sidney Fein*

Readers of Alan Walowitz's poems may find uneasy streets becoming easier, drab days becoming funnier, and troubled times more tolerable. His work teaches us that the irritation that seems to govern our relationships is really a lot like Love.

~ Sarah White, author of *to one who bends my time*

Alan Walowitz is a magnificent storyteller. Our everyday life is appropriate grist for his poetic pen—poems of power, poems of peace, poems to ponder.

~ Peter Wood, author of *The Boy Who Hit Back*

Alan Walowitz's poems speak to and for all of us: wisdom, mistakes, relationships, regrets, sadness and joy—hard earned lessons—what it means to be human and the humility that comes with it. Walowitz's sharp eye and skill as a poet will leave you with a flash of both recognition and admiration as he manages to capture small moments and intimate details that enrich and inform our lives.

~ Michael Minassian, author of *The Arboriculturist*

The Story of the Milkman

and Other Poems

ALAN WALOWITZ

TRUTH SERUM PRESS

The Story of the Milkman and Other Poems copyright © Alan Walowitz
First published as a book May 2019 by Truth Serum Press

BP#00078

All rights reserved by the author and publisher. Except for brief
excerpts used for review or scholarly purposes, no part of this book
may be reproduced in any manner whatsoever without express
written consent of the publisher or the author.
Any historical inaccuracies are made in error.

ISBN: 978-1-925536-76-8

Also available as an eBook / ISBN: 978-1-925536-77-5

Truth Serum Press
32 Meredith Street
Sefton Park SA 5083
Australia

Email: truthserumpress@live.com.au
Website: http://truthserumpress.net
Truth Serum Press catalogue: http://truthserumpress.net/catalogue/

Original cover photograph copyright © Jeanette Walowitz
Author photograph used by permission of the author
Cover design by and copyright © Matt Potter
Other images:
Page 21 – used by permission of Barry Bishop
Page 90 – https://www.jewishvirtuallibrary.org/
Page 113 – photograph used courtesy the Lucivero and Maraglino families
Back Cover – photograph by Alma Daza and used by permission of the author

 Truth Serum Press is a member of the
Bequem Publishing collective
http://www.bequempublishing.com/

For

my mother,
Esther Karp Walowitz
(April 26, 1919 – January 16, 2014)

and

my father,
Jeremiah Walowitz
(October 22, 1916 – February 19, 1987)

Contents

The Story of the Milkman   1

Coming Soon

Coming Soon	5
Lekhah Dodi	6
January the Tenth	7
Fallen Angel	8
A Kind Breeze	9
Brooklyn Bound	10
Sunrise Fire	11
Tremont	12
Waiting for Flowers	13
Moving Day	14
Roadkill	15
1938 Philco 4XX	16
The Infield Fly Rule	18
Video Postcard from Vietnam	20
Stress Test	22
Endings Set Us Free	23
Waiting for the Singularity	24

Role Models

"Lordy, I Hope There are Tapes"	29
Christmas Past with the Trumps	31
Role Models	32
Revision	34

Motion is medicine, you tell me	35
Guys like us	37
In Favor of Forgetting	39
Out for a Drive and Thinking about John Ferone	40
In the Company of English Teachers	42
Home of the Sages	44
String Theory	45
Experts	46
Don't Get Sick in America	47
A Dry Well	48
No Heat	50
Anthony Peter Tumbarello	52
Tony's Wake	53
Grace	54

Whatever Light is Left

Here	57
The Sequel	59
You Are Home	60
Last Dream of Morning	62
Marriage Song	63
Poem for the End of Daylight Savings	64
Photo of Snow in the Suburbs	66
The Golf Poem	68
Hailstorm	69
Divorce	70
Poem-a-Night	71
Night Drive with My Daughter	72
Metta Prayer	74
New Age Guy	76
Plumbing	77
Grownups	78

The Dark	80
System Restore	81

All That's Known

Before	85
Some Day	86
For Rosh Hashanah	88
Equinox	89
My Father Stops at Corners	90
How I Learned	92
Für Die Kinder	93
Raking	94
Button Trends—Summer 1959	96
My Father's Cake	98
A Cottage in Sag Harbor	99
Half-Life	100
Downsizing	101
The Cost of Bread	102
Remembering Ralph Edwards	103
All That's Known	104
Offerings for the Dead	105
My History in Valhalla	106

Coda

The Story of *The Story of the Milkman*	109
Acknowledgments	113
Thanks	117
About the Author	119
My mother wears a mask for Mardi Gras	back cover

The Story of the Milkman

When I was a kid our milkman was killed
right before dawn at a railroad crossing
one low whistle away from where we lived.
We read about it in the *Mirror*
and were in awe seeing Nick,
a man we'd actually met,
right there with the wife and kids he left,
inset with a picture of the wreck.
At bottom, a separate shot,
was the watchman, bleary and ashamed,
as he was led from the scene.
We grabbed our bikes and tore to the crossing,
but it was mostly cleaned up
except the street was closed
and if you wanted to cross
you had to ride all the way over to Farmers.
We just wanted to look.

Later, my father took us there in the car
and made a noise like a train coming through;
I dug my nails in my palms,
and wished Nick were my dad.
That's how strange crossings are:
you want the train to come
and kind of hope it won't.
I can't even see Nick's face anymore,
which I had memorized like a list of spelling words.
Or my father's, which I forgot to study at all.
The next week there was another milkman.
Then my father was gone
and I was a father.

What I hold onto most is that milk box
as if I owned it still
and Nick was going to fill it
with quarts of glistening glass.
Made of galvanized tin,
mottled from the weather,
you could barely make out the name
"Sheffield's" stenciled in red,
and on the hottest day of summer
it was so cold inside
you wished you could crawl in and hide
from whatever was confusing you to death,
or scaring you sick.

Coming Soon

Nothing lasts, and yet nothing passes, either.
And nothing passes just because nothing lasts.

Philip Roth

Coming Soon

Promised all winter off the whoosh and stagger of the LIE,
though an odd site for a farm stand, we agreed,
here in Queens among the row houses and abutting Mickey D's,
but the prospect of fresh fruits and veggies—
potatoes, sweet corn, raspberries in season,
from the rocky but fertile North Fork to those of us
starved from another long winter of cardboard cukes
and tomatoes that taste of too many late frosts—
was irresistible and well-worth the hope and wait.
How we mourned when the cross went up in spring,
triumphantly on top, blessed by a bishop in black,
and learned this Harvest Center trafficked only in souls
too tender yet to be reaped.

Lehkah Dodi
(Come, My Beloved)

*Sung on Friday night as Shabbat begins, to greet the Shabbat bride.
During the singing of the last verse, the entire congregation rises and turns
to the west towards the setting sun, to greet "Queen Shabbat" as she arrives.*

I have welcomed my beloved
too many times to think of this as new.
Yet here I am again, at what ought to be beginning,
back turned to the week, face to the door,
hardly richer for the settlements I have made,
the sum of all mistakes that've come before,
bills paid and too many left with a sigh, unopened.
The phone's rung off the hook unanswered and insistent
though your voice that follows so often
reminds me that my presence is long overdue
or, God forbid, no longer required.
I have heard you promise, the wretched week will fade to the past
but only until I hear the footsteps in the distance
that rise like a gentle wave on the beach at dusk, will I believe.
Ah, the subtle music, the fragrance, then open your eyes—
a celebrant she comes, and will I only have the will
to go and meet her, look beneath the veil
and ready myself to embrace the joy
that should be mine by birthright.

January the Tenth

after a painting by Tim Savage

In a far corner of the room, the Christmas decals,
peeling from the edges, but still enough intact
to reflect off the rain on the window,
retain some of the light of the season,
but only when the traffic signal so many floors below
changes from red to green and back again
in its predictable rhythm.

The gateleg table—so practical
the way it could hug a corner
and still seat sometimes five or six for holidays,
but not if they were too full-grown—
now's on its way to being antique,
though purchased new from a small shop in Buffalo,
soon after the war, when all seemed possible.
But the cards we place upon it
don't always want to remain upright,
though if they fall, we fix in passing,
without thinking much, even at this late date
when they'd just as soon be gathered up and tossed.

We've mostly forgotten who sent them,
as friends we've known grow farther away,
and many more each year exit our life and,
we only hope—how silence follows silence—not their own.
Though even this perpetual not knowing
can be a comfort, as time hurries by and another Christmas,
with any joy we've remembered to share,
dwindles in January's own sharp cold and unkind light.

Fallen Angel

from *The Daily Mail*, May 3, 2016

They have no internet; they don't know what a sex toy is,
comes the solemn report from Jakarta,
and *Only in the Banggai*, some will add,
looking down their noses at the fishers, who claim—
such ignorance!—they reclaim the land we tread,
each day they drag the sea.
But in the wake of the eclipse of the sun, they say:
The old gods can make anything happen:
A woman might float in the sea, and require our help,
this a test, perhaps—as the gods have commanded—
and surely have bestowed on us a Bidadari, an angel,
a sign from the heavens we dare not ignore—
and she—having all the requisite parts—
we clothed her for she is cold and wet
and we will worship at her feet for we are blessed,
and we will love our lady always, if sometimes in fits and starts.

Tell me in the west a man has never sailed upon the moon,
or has taken a dolphin for a mermaid, and a mermaid for a wife?
Nor have they whirled like the Sufis in their ventilating skirts?
Or the Na Nach who arrive uninvited on a Tel Aviv street
blaring techno from speakers on the roof of the van.
Though everyone looks askance; still everyone must dance.
And what of the passion of St. Thérèse Avila,
she of the bony finger now encased in glass
but could be of much use for such ecstasy
as is often required by faith and art?
So why not those meager ones, seldom smiled upon, or anointed
who mostly pull fish from the sea
and are happy to call it a living?

A Kind Breeze

After so much heat,
the clouds bear down
but refuse to rain.
Then a gift:
a kind breeze picks up
and you'd think the world was saved
the way the windows fly open
and breathing begins again
as if oppression were a rumor
finally nailed to the door.

Still, the oil gushes out of the ocean floor
just as we'd always prayed it would—
surely a sign that any gods
who haven't left town for the season
throw up their hands
and laugh at the willful way
we succor ourselves again.

So much for this life and the petty delusions
that make it work so well.
I'll take up with the breeze
and throw my hands in the air.
Not the madman next door
muttering how it's all gone to hell,
but one who's wise enough
to rise above the heat
and makes himself accessible
to assess damage, reconcile loss—
perfectly deaf to any wailing below.

Brooklyn Bound

after Julie Standig

Buff and bored, the long Latino Stanley Kowalski of the "F"
leans back in the hard seat as if he's in a hammock,
his legs stretched halfway across the car, and exclaims
what we might never otherwise suspect: *This is the life!*
Like a bowling ball, his well-pleased feet displace
the pins of *Going-to-Business Barbie,* complete with attaché,
who'd been holding the center bar in the crook of her arm
and managing still to waltz with *Marie Claire.*
She escapes with some high stepping
and makes for the guillotine door
as we follow with envious eyes, till she arrives,
winded but still exceedingly well put-together, in the car behind.
The rest of us, too timid to plan such escape, clear more space,
relieved to be omitted from Stanley's impressive reach,
if not his joie de vivre riding the "F",
as we bury ourselves in our electronic devices,
with those imagined messages from the world of the surface
we can't know for sure we'll ever emerge to receive.
The elderly Spanish woman on the other side
crosses herself with a mouthed *Dios mío,*
already retreated into The Bible she carries for such close calls,
maybe *Matthew 5:38* about offering your coat to the stranger,
or the one from *Ezekiel* about the Lord exacting vengeance.
Now the young man heads for the abandoned pole at center
and lifts himself parallel to the ground like a flag
and holds the position for a full count of three.
Impressed, but refusing to salute, I glance at la doña
for the sake of the camaraderie we now should share,
to which she shrugs, which indicates,
though I might well be from out-of-town,
that down here, under the ground, this is the life.

Sunrise Fire

August 1995

We were able to keep up so long
as the flame followed the old railroad tracks.
But when it leapfrogged Sunrise
and bounded deep into the Pine Barrens,
all hell broke loose.
Even the buck moth scattered and the white-footed mice
that eat acorns and pine seeds
and the red-eyed towhees and field sparrows,
with their bright pink bills from their nests.
We figured an act of God—the sun had baked the ground
where no rain had reached all summer,
and filled the floor with pine cones and oak leaves
which dry so easy and burn so well—
the way it brought with it this eerie quiet
as it blocked off access to the East End
the height of the season.

When the sun came up next,
the volunteers had all gone home
and the way the light bounced off the smolder and char
made it look lonely and lovely and ours—
no sudden pit stops, no emergency shopping,
no traffic whine taking up the silence.
But the sons-of-bitches and their wives,
and their kids and their European au pairs
must pray to more powerful gods—
they took to yachts, private planes, and helicopters.
And it came to pass the last weekend of summer
that some started to sow and rebuild and repair,
and others got where they were destined to go.

Tremont

A history buff, I grabbed the spot on Mayflower,
which I was certain I'd recall,
but would probably never find again
the way the streets wind around each other
and stop dead at the Hutch,
then you have to walk under the el on Westchester
where the streets tend to have new names
when you get to the other side;
or you make a wrong turn and get mesmerized
by the Thai bodegas that sell exotic flowers outside,
and Ecuadorian skin-treatment joints offering lava facials,
and the China Criolla with the combination plate
of chicken wings and fried rice and platanos for $4.95
which could keep you company while you're walking,
and soon find yourself at I 95,
which you can't get on anyway without a car,
but why would you want to
when you're looking for where you parked?
This part of the Bronx, Tremont, was born to be a wonderland
of hills and rills and rocky outcrops and kids climbing trees
but it's where Robert Moses bulldozed his way
right through people's kitchens
to create the promised land, mobile eff-ing America;
he'd make sure there were ways
—north, or west, or south—
for a guy with a car to get his ass out of the Bronx.
But now it's just a beautiful dream—
half the people only have the wheels on the bus,
which go round and round and take you
no farther than the city line,
and the other half can't even find where the hell they parked.

Waiting for Flowers

The married men who get in line have worked all day,
their weariness palpable and worn in rumpled overcoats,
though some are buttoned-down, but shoulders plenty slouched;
others, younger, maybe more upward-bound, tilt imperceptibly
toward the side they carry their attachés, heavy
with the same work lugged home the day before and before.
Though we promised we'd try to knock off early,
it's near 7:00 already and time's moving too fast and too slow
and the line's snaking out the door by now,
the ones at the end having replaced us—the poor suckers
we're glad to see so as to mark how far we've traveled
though we seem to have gotten nowhere quick—
even as the early-arrivers squeeze out past us,
their roses wrapped in wet paper, but clutched like treasure
the way men of old would bear their bounty safely into the dark.
Not much sound from us who wait; men don't say much.
It's cold enough for the cold to swallow even the sighs
that sometimes come unbidden.
Once, someone leaves the line
with a shrug that says, *Fuck it,* and the rest shake their heads
in awe at the homesick G.I. gone mad
who charges unarmed and naked into the sniper's nest.
We know this is where we must be, Valentine's Night,—
and we know the clock is ticking, maybe a nice dinner waiting,
the baby put down early, maybe candlelight, soft music,
who knows, a classic disk passed down from a long-dead uncle,
wine, a nice bottle, a gift from a neighbor,
but surely as we stand here, surely as the twenty in our fist,
there is an empty vase upon the table waiting.

Moving Day

She finishes the sweeping in front of the house
and moves on to the side. There the hose is in the way,
wound and wound in uneasy arcs on the cement path,
from just before when her husband—tired now and in to rest—
had been using it in the way of the suburbs,
powering into the street the smaller debris—cigarette ash,
blades of grass from a final cutting,
and Polly Noses from the old maple which leans now,
so many years later, out over the path.
When dry they tend to stick to the walk,
even clean as she works to keep it,
though it shouldn't much matter moving day.
In fact, I note to her, from my own driveway
next door where I'm trying not to watch too close,
but afraid I'll never see this scene again:
Millie, it's pretty damn clean.
Alan, I know. It's just . . . and her voice trails off.
Last thing I mean is to discourage her
and she goes to the back, now dragging her broom,
leans against the gate, sighs, as she looks at the place
her kids and neighbor-kids and grandkids played.
There had been a swing set, screams of joy
and sometimes pain, a plastic pool, grass
now covered over in concrete, less to maintain,
and says, only partly to me, turning to go,
I guess it's clean enough. For now.

Roadkill

The layers of late autumn—red, pale blue,
red again, then the black begins to ride up the horizon.
You might mistake for a flag of an invading army
that'll have you by the throat and won't let go
till another equinox appears and you can breathe again,
this time, perhaps, beneath a more forgiving sky.
Like when you finally—and against
your better judgment—say, *I love you*
to one so dear you'd even be willing to bear the silence
such a proclamation might inspire.
Then the voice of the Lady from Waze, seductive as a Siren,
wakes you soft and sweet, and without the heavy breathing
you'd counted on any time you used to be lashed to the mast,
and finds a new way to make you listen:
Roadkill on road ahead, she sings,
and there you are, looking for the corpse,
not feeling a bit like travelling through the dark, but for you
the hope of a chill down your front, the same as you get when
she tosses the word *love* at you, almost as if it were allowed.
There's expense in this, too, I suppose,
this figuring which lane the porcupine, slow, but determined
in his desire to cross all those lanes to meet his end,
then how to get close enough to avert your eyes from the mess:
the old push-pull, this fear of being so damn human
as to speak aloud the words you wish you'd learned to say easy.
But life's a bitch—even at 70—when you should know better.
So, you press the gas to the floor,
what you once called passing gear,
though damned if you want the road that remains
to pass you by quite so fast
as this.

1938 Philco 4XX

A shapely lady in heels,
tucks her legs modestly under,
but still enough akimbo to evoke faint possibility.
Dress demurely covers her knees
but her fanny casts a shadow like a seahorse.
Light-headed, and no wonder,
all this squatting to tune the radio
perched hip-high on spindly Queen Anne legs—
for that matter, her own might soon give way
to make ready for some swooping by a handsome man
come to save, if not herself, then her dignity
so she might reclaim her proper station.

Instead, here comes one with Churchillian bearing
who looks as if he'll never resume his position,
upright or otherwise, now that his trunk,
rendered nearly unsupportable,
has formed a permanent perpendicular
at the top of his legs.
His nose is firmly up against the dial as if to dare it
to remain distant and impossible to occupy
with the immobile and elephantine army
he's turned out to be.
The news from Dover is no better.

And now the mistress of the house
gives it a whirl, her glasses perched on her tiny nose.
Though her rump, challenging gravity,
remains improbably in the air
like a crane left the night by workmen,
and this contraption delicately counter-balanced by her ample bust.
Those ankles are not to be taken lightly
though her feet have been poured into dancers' shoes,
a final affectation from days
she'd rather not discuss but would if asked.
The call letters she's seeking
are from a faraway land and remain,
like the man she might have twirled with once on holiday,
so close at hand, but distant as a dream.

The Infield Fly Rule

... a fair fly ball which can be caught by an infielder with ordinary effort, when first and second, or first, second and third bases are occupied, before two are out ... the batter is automatically out. (Rule 2.0)

Once you accept that gravity
acts consistently on an object in motion;
and inertia can be conquered
even when they're your loggy legs
lifting you off the ground—
then in that odd, ordered universe
the Infield Fly Rule may seem just.

The full moon may strike you
dumb and limp and lost
when bat readies to encounter ball
and you hit it high as the moon—
still the ump declares, *You're out!*
before you've moved a step from home.

He must be right:
You didn't hit it far enough.
You don't deserve first
or the right to advance any runners.
But you've seen so many who are less
get to round the bases,
their arms making soaring motions
in the shadows of the moon,
their feet hardly touching the ground.

Some givens are fine
for mindless acceptance:
your heart pumping;
the moon tugging at the sea;
your eyes blinking imperceptibly
when a pretty girl passes on the street
and fails to notice you're alive.
But not now. Not this.

Let the shortstop let it drop,
dazzled by the beauty of your swing;
let the runners do-si-do
far from their base as they dare
before the jig is up;
let the batter take first unmolested,
nod his head in exaltation
then exit with a warm ovation.
So what if those who rule,
dressed impeccably
and schooled in the law,
can cite chapter and verse,
everything you've never deserved?

Video Postcard from Vietnam

This might have been the way it was
approaching rainy season in country.
The clouds grow ominous, layer upon layer,
on an otherwise perfect day on the river,
a signal for the wary to rustle an extra tarp or two,
though the carrying would be no delight,
as nothing had been then in the vicinity of Hue.

The water now takes on a faint smell of spoiled eggs
despite its reputation for pleasant odors when flowers fall.
The old ones will tell tourists who wonder about its name
that blood, having once troubled the riverbed,
forever taints the water that flows upon it—
the visitors nod having been made wise,
such wisdom not an industry brought often from the west,
though factories on either bank are artfully hidden
by scenes from a Disney transport—jungle rhythmically cooing;
water buffalo, slow-footed and harmless;
the too perfect remains of what might have been
an ancient French garden.

Now the husband and wife in the postcard
float down the Perfume River as if on a loop—
two people resting in lounges on a pleasure boat
that's been jury-rigged into seeming-junks topping the launches
that once plied the river and then were left behind.
There are those who miss them at home
and might question where they've gone.
Others have not seen them for some time
and might wonder why they're always here.
The odd, unspoken message says,
Here is a place we feel safe.
Their fingers barely touch across
the distance between them, the width of the deck,
as they try their best to make a heart of their hands.

Stress Test

One thing about a treadmill
is you don't get anywhere,
but you do it rather fast.
And if you stumble, as I'm prone,
never quite capturing
that left-right-left-right—
lub-dub, lub-dub, rhythm—
you might get to see the doc a little quicker
instead of waiting for results
with a roomful of less-than-perfect strangers
pretending to be engrossed
in *Cardiology Today*.

The med-tech, she warned me,
that I've got to keep up
or fall off the back of the hay truck.
That's the way she talked, this country girl
I kept flirting with to keep my mind off my heart,
moved to the big city to make her way,
but here she is with me,
stuck in another chilly room
without a single window to look out of
and onto any part of the world
I'm an hour closer to leaving
and she—after a long day with the likes of me—
might actually enjoy getting to know.

Endings Set Us Free

Call All County Vacuum
and they bring the big green truck
to clean up most everything—
fire, flood, petroleum spills—
but not this botched goodbye,
messy enough to qualify for special rates,
and oddly without the usual junk and detritus
that by rights we ought to be able to call on
to salve each I've-been-wronged,
or to look back on fondly one day
with a heartfelt but quizzical, why did I care?
as it's swept out with the old year's dust.

Let's take this drift into full estrangement
and make it work for us.
You could live a long time,
the Flying Dutchman of the cyber oceans,
everybody's BFF;
or here I am, patiently awaiting
the next Transit of Venus—
true, not due till next century,
but if I insist on seeing it, I'll have to hang on;—
so what if I'll feel bad all the while,
crane my turkey neck to the sun
then go completely blind.

Waiting for the Singularity

We have the means right now to live long enough to live forever ...
But most baby boomers won't make it ...

Raymond Kurzweil

Like Moses denied the Promised Land,
we weren't built for the world to come
where machine and man are one.
The parade will begin without us,
as those who leave us joyfully behind
toss their walkers and canes
as if Our Lady had landed like Dorothy
on their former, miserable selves
and they begin what's called
Forever.

Soon our loss will be but
a few lines in dusty textbooks:

> *Everything began to fail.*
> *Their tongues searched*
> *for words they'd never find.*
> *Their penises wouldn't obey.*
> *All their parts wilted just that way*
> *and soon they were bound*
> *for the analog museum.*

So while we're still able,
let's gather at the Church of the Born-Too-Soon,
receive each other at the table
and set in order the things that are on it:
our tired laurels, ill-gotten gains,
and the mess of the world we've made.
We won't have the bounty of endless time
to repair, but there will be oh so many
to share our labors with.

Role Models

Unhappy the land that is in need of heroes.

Bertolt Brecht

"Lordy, I Hope There are Tapes"

James Comey, June 8, 2017

You call up the stairs to tell me what we'll need
to make it through the long night ahead.
The water's running and I can hardly hear,
though you're known to assert
that to listen and to hear were never the same.
No matter, we know this part always ends
in a caustic, *Nevermind.*
I do hear you slam the door
and imagine your short sigh before heading off into your day.

I'm alone now and can make mine any way I'd like—
though, Lordy, I hope there are tapes
for later when I get to the grocery
and this great forgetfulness is bound to come over me,
surrounded by the bounty of America:
shelves stacked with goods
no one could ever use, given even a lifetime;
the produce shaped into so many pyramids
we'd once hoped to visit, but now know we never will;
the prepared foods, chilled, and ready
to be reheated and consumed
but where should we put them if left uneaten
when our day is done?

This is a great land with so many choices
of who to believe and why, and infinite possibilities of what to buy,
so please don't berate me when I call
to ask what I need to bring.
I know we already have everything
and are likely still to feel we've been taken, and underserved,
and finally, and fatally, misunderstood.
Though, Lordy, I hope there are tapes
of the long night so long ago
when we first fell into each other's arms.

Christmas Past with the Trumps

The Q17 would take me past Jamaica Estates—
though I didn't know then of Trump,
whose pop already was a big deal in Brooklyn,
but I knew this was where the rich folks lived.
And I'm sure young Donald, though a bully even then,
wasn't the one who pushed me aside
and shook me down for a couple of dimes
in the arcade at the Jamaica Terminal
just to get at the shooting range,
with a rifle that shot light at the little metal ducks that
would shut with a snap like a flock of cheap valises.
A guy like him didn't take the bus, I learned,
and would have pocketsful of dimes to fill his own machines
that lined his basement finished in teak and kingwood—
and had real guns to shoot at summer camps
with riflery and riding, Western and English,
and cloth napkins that came with service
and they didn't dare call it mess.

My father would drive us through Trump's part of the world
this time of year, to see the Christmas lights of the rich,
and we probably went by his house a couple of times,
though the well-to-do never put up lights,
while the newly rich installed just one color—
a melancholy blue—on their mansion's outer edge
so passersby like us might be awed by its size,
in the winter dark, while the family
that might have lived inside was off on a cruise,
though they likely left the curtains open,
and the white lights shaped like candles on the huge tree
would illuminate those ten-foot ceilings,
in those cavernous front rooms that otherwise
were never permitted to reveal
even a shadow.

Role Models

"President Trump delayed on Thursday evening the release of thousands of pages of classified documents related to the John F. Kennedy assassination ... The president allowed the immediate release of 2,800 records by the National Archives, following a last-minute scramble to meet a 25-year legal deadline."

Washington Post, October 27, 2017

I was in homeroom when JFK got shot
and we weren't told much
about what'd happened—
or about much else—
this was high school, late shift,
and the afternoon wore
so damn slowly into night.
But that day I learned
from the very purposeful
and well-dressed Mr. Wulf
that life must go on
and a greater angle of a triangle
is opposite a greater side,
and though I never had the need
to read the Warren Report,
I hear those august guys
absolutely nailed Theorem #6
with their fine discussion and diagrams
of angles and distance from the Book Depository
to the limo riding by in Dealey Plaza
carrying a human god, the man we most admired,
though we later found out
he had feet of clay and was just a guy.

I also learned that
if a teacher remains in the back of the room
and tamps down weeping to a quiet, plaintive sob,
a tough old bird like Mrs. Hirsch in English
can wring a pink handkerchief dry
then drown it again with her tears
and no one will think less of her.
Though the president we've got now
makes me sick with his lies,
his ugliness, and everything else he hides,
there's nothing left in the vault,
unrevealed from 1963 or '64
that could have taught me any better
what kind of grownup
I ought to hope I'd grow up to be.

Revision

You must change your life, Rilke said.
But what did he know about moving toward a fence
in such ragged order, armed with rocks and kites,
where live arms will greet you,
their 19-year-old bearers trained in this same theater
and are in receipt of their rules of engagement
and memorized the battle plan
like lines in a drama where the outcome is certain,
which will only make the ending more rich, more real?
Yet, how can you tell what these supernumeraries will feel
once the curtain comes down, and the dead
are not mannequins and are moved instead
to the theater of the ground?

Much like this nation where I'm told,—
even if I'm the son unable to ask—
I can return any time I'd like,
I've been on this earth the allotted three score and ten.
I assure you, from vast experience,
to change a life requires more than one's full portion.
But to revise, to see yourself again,
that can be an everyday miracle, if only we'd try.
Some of our fathers tell us we're not quite chosen,
but just to be certain, we had better be better
and a light unto the nations.
This is hard work, the toughest there is,
but, didn't I hear God say, in some unrecorded verse,
Hey, pal, isn't this what you signed up for?

Motion is medicine, you tell me

and other times you say, *Medicine is motion*,
and when I fail to apply the commutative property
and switch it back around,
you tell me I'm being difficult
which I'm known to be
when I don't really give a shit,
and forget the Prime Directive:
In marriage, it's best to go along to get along.

It also shows that day to day, Yeats was wrong:
Things don't fall apart;
they just get confused and eventually misshapen
till you can't figure which end is up,
or what's the subject of the sentence,
or even which of the seven classic disciplines we ought to apply
that would bring meaning to a challenging concept.
This could explain Brexit, or the National Front in France
—*Liberté, Egalité, Fraternité*, my ass—
or Pres. Trump's one nation under God—*Trust me*, he says:
we'll have the very best One;
or the existence of the God particle
which sounds so promising
that something—anything—might be holding us together.

I've learned reading *Physics for Dummies*
that a body in motion tends to stay in motion,
though I've noticed it's plenty easy
these days to tumble into an easy chair and fall fast asleep
with hardly a moment's notice, even with all the bad news
on loud and in a continuous loop.
It was said Dali, himself, preferred to nap with a pie-tin on his head.
When it would fall and crash like cymbals on the hardwood floor
he would wake to the alarm, now rested,
wax his moustache again, and get back to work.
I guess, given current conditions,
we'd be wise to forego our next nap,
and get our asses back in gear.

Guys like us

Jamaica, NY 1973

I wasn't exactly Teacher of the Year,
but classes were small and that limited the damage.
A lot of kids never came to school
except for lunch some days and always the last of the month
when free bus passes were handed out
—then there was Title One, LBJ's bonanza
which would have made things more right—
except for guys like us. No matter.
Our failures would lead to full employment in some jungle
where too many of these kids were headed—
so guys like us agreed to hunker down behind a desk
from 8 to 3 in this godforsaken neighborhood
to avoid a free tour ourselves and a tent in some rice field
by sending someone else's kid in our place.
Still, some of us made sad jokes about our petty classroom trials:
At least in Nam they give you a gun,
we told each other at a bar after school,
or smoking weed way too far into a night
that would become dawn and a day
we'd slog through in shades as if the hallways were the jungle,
our heads pounding, and handed out
word searches, crosswords, and rebuses—
whatever it would take for guys like us to make it through.

It felt faraway this damage I inflicted
till the morning Clifford Glover, age 10, was shot by a cop
when walking with his pop to work
through an empty lot just a mile away—
and then I knew the game was up.
George Mackie, that kid didn't know to get out of the rain,
and used to say he preferred to sit under the flag
so he could do his work "under justice,"
looked at me different from then on
and didn't want to hang around my room during lunch
and, whether true or not,
I swear I saw him eyeing me each afternoon
as the cops escorted us to our cars which would take us home,
to a neighborhood safe for guys like us.
None of this makes me proud
but like the doctor I'd never grow up to be
I lived by the rule: First, do no harm
and I figured none of what I did or didn't would amount to much
especially compared to what living was bound to do.

In Favor of Forgetting

Jamaica, NY, 1973

If ever I mistook myself for a teacher,
there was Cassandra
in the middle row, first seat
and smack in front of my face
to remind me otherwise.
Even after a year separating subjects from verbs,
counting syllables in words she couldn't pronounce,
and this white-boy-come-to-the-ghetto
reading from *Famous Myths and Legends*
he was sure would save her
from the world falling apart before our eyes—
the sacking of Troy, false promises from the gods,
a life that would be less, no matter how she wailed.
She'd call me *Mr. Thing*, claimed
she couldn't remember my name.
But what if it turns out
refusing to remember
is the very thing you need
to get you through this life?

Out for a Drive and Thinking about John Ferone
(1943-2003)

I got to Millbrook twelve years late,
though the horsey set was still sunning itself in the cafés,
their Lexuses polished to a nub
and tied to the decorative posts at the curb.
John had died before he and I could take up golf,
or watch birds with the Audubons
dragging their fancy Wellies through the mud,
or cash in any of his hoped-for lottery winnings—
though plenty well-off already,
a bachelor, who taught the hell out of those kids even in the summer
and drove a bus each afternoon, and never spent much,
as if the Great Depression he'd been taught as a kid
was right around the next curve on Fisher Avenue.
Fridays the dollar tickets were stuffed
in the top pocket of his Dacron shirt,
the same one he'd worn, stained and askew,
since he was a pup, and the principal took a chance on him,
despite the way he dressed and his plentiful unpolished ways:
John was born rumpled and called *not so smart* from the first—
no one had yet heard him declaim Romeo's lovesick soliloquies
and make them make sense to thirteen-year-olds
who had plenty of problems of their own,
or convince the motley kids he taught
why they'd rather tour Sunnyside

than spend and get at the Mickey Ds right off the highway
close in to the old Sleepy Hollow cemetery
where I bet John would have wished to be buried,
though the Babe and Gentleman Jimmy
are now his neighbors up in Hawthorne.
How fitting for an ill-fitting squire from Millbrook.
Still, years later, strangers come up to tell me
he was their perfect teacher,
though I know for a fact John had plenty of faults.
I just can't think of any right now.

In the Company of English Teachers

There are better ways, I suppose, to spend one's days:
above the battle between those who mourn
Old Gerund's passing
and those who kick dirt on his grave;
between those who seek a kinder, gentler tome and those
who'd as soon see little Piggy skewered
just to remind how kinder, gentler we are not now
but maybe could be
if only we would read.

But me, I'll take what I've found here
beyond the din of logarithms
that couldn't help anyone
out of the forest of his grief
on a cold and lonely night.
Here, history is not allowed to lie—
as in those books of purported fact,
when what really happened is incontrovertible:
Huck and Jim keep floating past Cairo
again and again. Here, broken beakers, (which,
I hypothesize, speak only in shards of truth)
won't ever cause a broken heart.

In times of despair, I myself have wished to
scatter those balls in the gym,
holler, *Play!* and proudly proclaim
some battle was won on the playing fields
of Eton, where our mother tongue
lies gasping. But surely not here.
Here, among us, we have made a place
where even those old and out of breath
might settle in and for a time
make a home not only out of words,
but of what they're worth.

Home of the Sages

On the ever-growing list of What I Never Knew
comes word that the Great Ali's grandson becomes Bar Mitzvah;
and watch as the Eagle Eye Home Inspection Service
pulls into the empty spot next to the hydrant—
then spreads its stainless-steel wings like the phoenix,
and morphs into a Mitzvah Mobile, ready to do all kinds of good.
And waiting for me this morning on the front stoop, this:
The New East Side Nursing Home—on Bialystoker off Willett
a short walk, from the Essex Street Station, if you got the legs,
turns out to be the Home of the Sages.

But that's how it is with Sages—
you never know where they'll turn up.
You might happen on one in a coffee shop,
head bowed and shuckling over the puzzle in the Times;
or another gets loose and goes weaving up the street,
mumbling everything he knows of the Talmud
to no one in particular. It couldn't hurt,

but better to find them where they gather each day
in Loisaida, soon after daybreak, from who knows what walkup,
having already taken their tea
through a cube of sugar clenched between their gums
and now they're limping, some with canes and walkers,
up the ramp and into the first-floor meeting room
of that rat-trap, the New East Side Nursing Home—
then counting each other to a dozen most days.
Who should care so long as they make it to ten?
Or if they have to—not for nothing, these are Sages—
one goes to the landing and hollers up the stairs:
Rodriguez, Ven aca. Por favor. ¿Su Madre era judia, no?
We got to make minyan.

String Theory

When the wise Bhante Wimala tied this Sai Sin bracelet
round my wrist, he called for protection and peace,
then chanted the traditional Buddhist blessing
as if he really meant it,
which, unlike me, is the only way he knows.

Ever since, I've had a throbbing back,
a digestive tract that hardly works at all,
and an aching heel
that would make Achilles's mom
feel pangs of guilt all over again.

Bhante, I said, let us untie and start again,
since, despite your best intention, these strings,
wound and bound so well, won't work.
Now, more Jewish mother than guru, he avers,
Alan, leave them be. Things could be worse.

Me, I bowed my head, if not in obeisance,
at least out of respect, for what I can't embrace
but find, of a sudden, I've come to own:
The peace and protection of knowing for sure,
no matter how ungraceful, I'm growing old.

Experts

September 5, 2014

Still no sign of the big jet from Malaysia,
but this other little flight has gone mute over the ocean,
and the excitement on Cable is palpable.
A private plane, private folks on board,
and we're tracking it live like it was OJ,
after what is reported by some, who claim to know,
to be an insidious leak in the fuselage and hypoxia setting in,
the pilot slumped over the instruments,
the lone passenger dozing in her seat.
Not a bad way to go, perhaps,
compared with having your throat cut
by a clean, sharp blade in the desert, and then your head hacked off
with the serrated edge, while the blood spurts from your carotid.

Funny what passes for occupation these days—
Others, and let's give them their due and call them Experts,
will study the video for clues as to the accent of the killer,
homing in on East London Ethnic; others will practice
the latest art and science of vein-matching
of his foolishly ungloved hands,
and others, still, will study the engineering of the blade.
Hey, dead is dead, but that's what Cable doesn't care to remind us
while counting on the next shoe to drop:
the next guy kneeling in the desert,
the next plane dropping from the sky.

Don't Get Sick in America

Despite not being a doctor, I give him my best advice:
AARP, I tell him. *Always, At all costs, Remain Perpendicular.*
My old pal Willard would laugh if his hearing aid hadn't come loose
and we'd been sitting at the diner,
shooting the breeze over coffee, him telling me the same story
the third or fourth time. I love the guy.
But now he's lying on a gurney in the ER corridor
the 4th straight hour, getting edgy, and who can blame him
after all this time, and against my best advice,
he's parallel to the floor along with all the others,
quiet on their gurneys or writhing gently in pain,
even the pain-energy wrested out of them?
They're black and brown and grey and young
and the doctor—who hurries by from time to time
gives me a look that signifies, *I know, I know, it's crazy*—
she's a beautiful yellow-beige, with a face shaped like a heart
and I think I'm in love. The ER, this is America,
the great equalizer, no one's special here, no one
gets to see the doctor first because he's middle class or white,
or he used to be a Protestant from Rochester back in the day
and he was famous for clicking his heels and saying,
In Germany they stand up when I enter the room!
And everyone would tell him, *Sit down and shut up, Willard!*
Though I'm not next of kin,
a nurse figures I must be close, so stops by and tells me,
he'll have a stress test first thing in the morning,
after spending the night in the hall
cause the treadmill's booked the rest of today.
And just in case you needed a reminder,
Don't get sick in America,
you gotta have patience to burn,
and one way or another, you're gonna have to pay.

A Dry Well

After all this rain, the water's settled in
at the bowed-end of the lot
where it always seems to find a home.
Tool belt cinched, flashlight in hand,
I wade in to clear the muck,
struggle to pry the cap
which hasn't been dislodged for years,
while the water provides
a cold reminder against my boots
of one more thing I can't manage to do.
I take the auger to the drain,
let the cable pay out
and nothing moves except the neighbor—
an old guy with bad ticker,
I was sure would give out this winter,
who's emerged from his wet grave to watch me fail again.
Finally, he hollers, *It don't lead nowhere,*
as if I should have known all along
what he's taken his sweet time to say.

So this time there's nothing to be done,—
no artery to peer into with a light,
no catheter to push through,
no stent to be set,
no valve to replace,
no ventricle to stir,
no auricle to put your ear to and hear.
Just wait till the rain lets up
and the water finds a place below,
in the heart of things we can never see,
but where we'll spend our time
calling to those above
all the ways they've managed to fail.
It's a dry well, he shouts to me.
Not that it matters what our failures are called.

No Heat

Leo didn't want much for the work,
but when offered the keyboard
that lay doused in cellar dust—
same shit had wrecked his lungs a lifetime
and now caused this clogged,
syncopated samba, to come from the place
his voice box should be—he packed it up,
wheezed, *Good Night, Ahl,*
and was gone for good.

I call him every day to finish the work,
mend the pipe still leaking—no answer,
till one night he turned up in a dream.
But you know dreams; you can't remember
what they were by the time you wake—
though Leo liked to say
you could dream an answer to anything:
string theory, *No problame;*
nuclear fusion, *Here is how you do;*
the way to reroute the pipe
that's in the way of the life you really want.

Now when I open the closet
Leo built tight as a casket,
I swear I hear the rhythm of old Porto Alegre,
picked out by two fingers
pulsing back and forth on the keys,
puk shhhu, puk shhhu, puk shhhhu,
the drip of hot water on frozen floor,
and the steam that comes.
The sound could drive you nuts,
unless you choose to shut the door.
Or close your eyes and dream it gone—
along with every little thing you tell yourself
shouldn't mean this much to you.

Anthony Peter Tumbarello

Where your spine or mine
squared with our legs
when mothers told us
to sit straight in our chairs,
Tony's listed more than a bit.
When we walked
other kids would stare
and sometimes strangers'd
cross the street to inquire,
Son, what's wrong with your friend?
as if Tony couldn't hear
for being so bent.
I was an embarrassed kid,
but he was already a man,
fourteen years old
and full-grown by then—
four-six, at least.
Tony would crane his neck
in defiance, and stretch
all the way to four-foot-seven,
just so he might
politely suggest:
Drop dead, lady,
or
Fuck you, sir.

Tony's Wake

Anthony Peter Tumbarello (1945-1974)

His body, curled in life,
fit easy in the full-sized box.
A man wouldn't stand for one
cut for a kid and, God forbid,
made death seem airy and light.
I'd never been to a wake before
but you hear of the work morticians do.
Peeking in his casket
I half expected
the kiss of death
to turn the little toad he was,
my old pal, into a prince,
crowned and all aglow:
no longer a virgin,
lips puckered and set for a kiss
or at least to whistle a tune.
How about little Tony
finally, straight and tall?
But, Death, even you,
in your high falutin' majesty,
you couldn't uncurl him after all.

Grace

Seems not quite right to trouble a little girl
with that stately-lady name.
But, sure enough, someone did,
in hopes, maybe, she'd grow into a willowy tree
or the gentlest rain.
But it's Gracie—for now—two long vowels make for
a name she can wrap her mouth around.
Though the preacher says,
There's nothing Now about Grace—
It's like the rain that cometh—or doesn't—
from nothing said, or done or, even, prayed.
We've just gotta wait on the Lord.
But what if it takes more than the time we've set aside,
or the time He's allotted,
or ends up being, as promised, but like the rain
the time we didn't want it,
rumbling against our arrival at the beach,
a short stay we'd long planned
against life's frequent confusion,
bikes and chairs strapped to the car,
with no promise of surcease up ahead
and, the way we've packed,
no hope of seeing what's coming from behind?
Or we get none out west where we need it most,
while the almond-growers are squeezing the last ounce
from the ground like a mop wrung dry.
Whatever it is, He'll give it to us anyway,
but in His own good time.
Still, *How sweet the sound*, the President sings,
and despite any doubts I keep to myself,
I'm sure that makes little Gracie happy—
she saw him once on *Sesame Street*.

Whatever Light is Left

*Writing has laws of perspective, of light and shade
just as painting does, or music.
If you are born knowing them, fine.
If not, learn them.
Then rearrange the rules to suit yourself.*

Truman Capote

Here

for Jeanette

To get me to go
where I don't want to go,
my wife will say,
We're here and we're here, which means
I ought to get my ass out of the car
and not make her waste another trip.
Or *here* turns out to be a damn lie
as she points to the map *here* and *here*
which are where she really wants to go.
In any case, I don't want to hear
some rainy middle-of-the-night:
Why can't I ever get where I want?—
which breaks my heart
and makes me mad enough to scream,
What about me? Instead,
I go back to sleep.

Of course, getting *here*
the car gets stuck in a ditch,
or nuclear winter breaks out on the way,
or the radio reports the death
of still one more famous Jew
we didn't even know.
But she knows me and knows I would feel
so much better about everything
here inside our own four walls.
Truth is, nothing much ever happens,
but if it did, she'd say,
It happened and it happened.
Or, *You have so much to learn
and you're running out of time.*
Or, this good old heartbreak:
You call this living?

The Sequel

They will call him brave.

'Penelope', Dorothy Parker

The universe is telling us plenty—and some of it true—
but what to do with all the conflicting information?
These days I lash myself
to practiced habit and established form.
You'd be surprised
who'll watch a guy muck about in quicksand
when he hardly gives a shit at all.
Sometimes I stop and browse
the cards and letters you fans send.
I like the ones that read like fortunes best:
Don't seek so hard.
Settle down.
Feel free to be old. And even more poetic:
Come joyfully to the fruits of home.
What you've read or heard
might have once been true:
the glossy smile of native girl on travel brochure
could send me hot and frenzied
in an entirely new direction.
But I always choose Ithaca now—
hapless suitors, wife gone grey,
son who doesn't know me.
Cowardly? I admit, but comfort of a kind
what love and duty will have us do.

You Are Home

My father paces the lobby of the Hotel Le Monde, a little outside of Brussels. The prints, in the style of the late Flemish school, stare down at him, but the people inside them are too busy, too joyful in their village life to engage the lonely soldier come to set them free. The war sputters to a close a few hundred miles to the east and my father lights one cigarette after another and crushes each, half-smoked, beneath his impatient heel. He is lost inside, his buddies upstairs, for them the war brought closer to an end in the arms of the *jeune filles*, who wear their boredom like the cheap perfume in their hair. The world will be appeased that they can hardly see themselves in each others' eyes, the light failing outside, the lamps dimmed by elegant rags torn from more innocent days, now too painful to recall.

My father stares at the clock hanging crooked on the wall. The time is not right, but he allows himself to think of his wife and daughter who wait for him on the other side. He wishes he knew them. For all his jokes, his practiced ease, he knows little of women and the world they make. But he is certain where they are is home, and he wishes he were there, and he wishes he had not come to this place which has only made him more lonely, more certain that something unnamed and terrible will happen, that he will miss his own life, that he will never be home.

And I am his son a lifetime later and have finally been born.
I have wandered from woman to woman and you laugh and say
I'm like a man looking for a home. Some nights I even dream
myself standing at your door. It is already dawn and I can
hardly remember the dangers of the battlefield, the mines I have
dodged, the unsteady rat-tat-tat of the gunner at my heels.
I ring your bell and ring and ring, but you never answer. For all
my false bravado, my derring-do, I cannot knock, I cannot
demand, I cannot beat down your door, though I know, and
have always known, you are home.

Last Dream of Morning

The god who'll wake with a stretch and yawn
watches fully detached
as the boat tumbles over the falls.
No start, nor thrum of the coming to
in the striped light of day,
shivering off the shock of the gurgling river—
Now washed ashore, naked,
nearly drowned, he finds himself
late for work, unable to utter a sound.
How painful to be saved this way:
though awake, and finally abroad,
still not taken for alive.

Marriage Song

After years huddled together, and some may note,
joined at the hip, you might begin to take after
the matted, mangy mutt whose now grizzled nape
you love to stroke as you watch TV, cuddled
beneath the afghan, the two of you, cozy and warm,

knowing you'll never resemble your wife quite the same,
she who refuses your unspoken plea
to make herself over in your image: *Let's sport
matching yellow argyles together, perfect for autumn weather*—
as you'd walk each other jaunty and proud down the boulevard.

Nor will she go willingly to pot after watching your belly grow
far beyond the little love handles that had once
been endearing—and, truth be told, prompted giggles
as she tried them out and got plenty good
holding on and yelling *yippee ki yay*.

Though time to time, you do detect in her that cross-eyed stare
you've perfected in place of anger, or leave-me-the-hell-alone,
but thank God never that hangdog look you try
when you want food, or sex, or pity,
and she looks at you sideways instead and warns:

Watch it, Buddy, you'll end up alone and hungry at the pound.

Poem for the End of Daylight Savings
(November 1, 2015)

One way to control camel crickets is to adopt a cat ...
Felines are fascinated by crickets' hopping motions and will hunt them.

Networx.com

It was kind of you to offer to do the laundry,
though I know the basement bugs make you nuts.
The exterminator said these camel crickets
head inside this time of year for warmth—just like us,
and probably through the cracks in the storm cellar door.
We haven't used it in years, so why not?
And now that they're comfortable
they're bounding in and out of the sheets
and onto the speckled basement floor
then back again, a playground for the uninvited.
But the cat, perched near the window, hears my voice
telling him, *These are some hoppy bugs!*
and wonders if the world is losing its way,
the air and some sun still streaming in at him in November,
and opens, then closes one quizzical eye,
to recall that the pun is the lowest form of wit—
and he's got better things to do his age, than chase a bug
who's got no interest in being caught and torn asunder.

So where else could this poem head but here,
on the Day of the Dead—and what's worse
this Return to Standard Time,
free daylight done for now when we need it most
as the sun makes its way—I don't give a damn
what science may say; like the Ancient I am, I believe what I see—
a little quicker each day to the western horizon?
I know the cat doesn't care—
he's a metaphor for me;
and for all I know that's all I am for him: It's only fair.
But if I make it through one more winter, I swear

I'll chase those damn camel crickets myself
around the basement floor and out the storm cellar door.
Then promise I'll pause to take the warm spring breeze—
to hell with the laundry, and all the chores—
and spend more time with you
to bathe in whatever light is left.

Photo of Snow in the Suburbs

The snow that began the night before fell far into the day,
leaving just enough time as the moon rises,
so we can take in some of that utter whiteness
before the cars are unshovelled and their leavings get stirred in
with all the ugly kinds of mess humans can make.
But for now, the snow tops the neighbor-evergreens
like a row of strollered infants in sun bonnets
sleeping softly at the park; streets still glitter
where the plows haven't hit bottom
and left a coat of ice for tomorrow morning's melting;
no one's out except for us who had been house-bound
and stir-crazy for a night and day of too much TV, too much wine,
and the never quite suppressed fear built into us humans
that we'll never get anywhere again.
But here on the street the air seems cleaner somehow
that way it gets after some little cold sun
warms everything just enough to help our lungs work easy
and make us swear we'll swear off drink and the great indoors.
You say you want to try to get a picture of it all—
the moon, the street, the snow caps, the air, the evergreens—
and you climb to the top of the pile of snow
some shoveling's made into a modest mountain.
Always the arbiter of what's impossible,
I'd tell you it can't be done, but you're determined
and I wait patiently at the door
instead of rushing inside where I'd prefer.

There's no danger out tonight—by now plenty of moonlight—
even the raccoons that get more brazen each night
are tucked beneath the porches and into our basement wells.
I too want to take it all in, as you angle for that picture—
destined never to be looked at again,
you know I would be happy to say.
But mine would just be you
and I will keep it in memory's well where
what's truly impossible might finally find the place
where it can permanently reside.

The Golf Poem

The golf links lie so near the mill
That almost every day
The laboring children can look out
And see the men at play.

Sarah Cleghorn, *The Golf Links*

My wife says *J'accuse* partly in jest.
She means: *You get lost on the golf course—*
or was it a woman?
I figure she ought to be happy
not having to see me fastened to the desk
troubling the 23rd version of this poem no one will read
because golf's a waste of good time
and perfectly useful space
and there's no poetry in it.

I like to spend time in it alone,
make my way the order I want,
which is fine so long as I don't hold up play.
No one cares what you do in poems,
but golf doesn't like when you break the rules.
I try to walk gingerly there.

My wife wishes I'd care as much about the yard.
She insists, *You can't make a poem from golf,*
but you can take a scythe
to the weeds out back and wield it like a 7.
I never tell her how in school we had to memorize *The Golf Links*,
and old Mrs. Koehler made us boys promise
not to take up that cold, stupid game—
and the girls never to marry
any frozen idiot who did.

Hailstorm

August 1, 2011

The rages of recent days settle upon us,
grow into practical comforts:
those we'd trusted to allay the silence are silent;
one-time lovers barely recognized in the hall;
what might have been called kindness once
—a nod as we pass, a door noiselessly latched,
S*uch a handsome tie*—become particular annoyances.
As is this sudden sun, the way it nudges us unwilling
into a mood we've lost the context for.

So let's remember with nostalgia just yesterday
when the rain turned to hail the size of lab rats,
translucent, fat and blind—
they made that scurrying rat-tat-tat on the roof
and those death-defying dents in the parked cars
and even the ones trying to escape
though there was nowhere to go.

It's harsh weather that could comfort those
who lose sight of what life is about—
ducking shards when the glass shatters about us
even in the so-called safety of our homes.
Here's real running through the rain
and not even vaguely romantic.
The drops, suddenly so visible,
might turn out to be much less hazardous
to our long-term health and well-being.

Divorce

She woke with the Yiddish *opgetn* on her lips,
a word she hadn't heard since she was small
when spoken late at night in the hushed kitchen
of a railroad flat on the Lower East Side
as she pretended to be asleep in the next room—
it was always better to listen,
better to know.
When I got home late that night our bed was gone,
taken apart slat by slat, rail by rail,
and shipped into the future which,
though often unremarkable, is always unknown.
Ordinarily, she didn't trust in dreams,
but to be taken by surprise
she never would allow.

Poem-a-Night

Since the good poems have all been written
someone's got to find the ones left behind.
Arise, you seekers of the poems of desperation,
it's four a.m., high time to stagger, sober-drunk
from pillow to post, poet on the prowl,
and into my daughter's room
where the music might entertain the dead
and every light is on.

And there she is asleep, naked the waist down
with Mac alive and grinning on her lap,
the images of cheap reruns playing
on her thighs and in her dreams
and even at that hour
her friends are vying to let her know the news:
who's grounded for life
and who broke up with whom.

I avert my eyes and stumble out
managing only to shut the lights.
What more could I do,
her lap dancing and dinging?
We're only poets
and daughter-rearing is a useless distraction
that keeps us from the poems
that have long been promised
in our sorry covenant with a vengeful lord.

Night Drive with My Daughter

She's late—God knows for what—
and you're stuck behind another damn truck
on the Staten Island Expressway.
You've tried everything to calm her
but nothing you say is what she wants—
your very existence makes her mad
and why the hell not?

She's sprawled in back and leans against the door,
though you've told her again she might fall out
and you've loved her so much.
Her headphones make her deaf to any appeal
and more dear to you now as a consequence,
her imperfections suddenly undisguised,
human and forgivable,
and not having been visited upon her
by the same foreign power
that brought her her womanly body and wild hair.

This is not exactly what you'd hoped
starting out, and certainly not here in Staten Island,
the cheap malls where no one ever goes
built on our own shit and rusted bumpers
and bustling with the busyness of zombies
who you'd accept as means to an end
because it might never get better than this,
the truck falling over on you as you pass
just to leaven the silence
and your brains chewed up while waiting for the cops
and the two of you rising together holding hands
the way it was when she was four,
and now finally forgiving your sins,
and though you haven't spoken of it for years
you arrive some place like heaven
because it's something you both can understand,
since nothing else makes sense
and maybe you could stand each other there
and be together again.

Oh, and long as we're dreaming,
let's make it a beautiful view
of the sun coming up over Brooklyn,
as the truck we're tucked behind rattles and reels
and the wind winds you up on the overpass,
your day-old coffee sloshing in the Styrofoam cup,
your daughter weeping in back,
her head gently keeping time to what she feels
and what, from this time on, you,
of all people, are never to know.

Metta Prayer

One polite handshake and already she knows
my chakras are out of alignment
and I'd better get them aligned and quick.
She starts on my crown: *Violet*, she claims.
Not virile enough for the likes of me,
but what could one so young know
of my particular brand of manly?
Then she works her way slowly down
to the area where my third eye
ought to be; I try hard to see—
and though I've never known from indigo,
her hands are cool like a field of blue flowers.
She sprays me with fragrant oils
that might make more tolerable
the faint smell of derision and doubt
that always seems to surround me.
She's working too hard,
but what choice does she have
having chanted, and so sincerely—

> *May all beings be whole and be healed;*
> *May all have whatever they need—*

I've kept my spine straight enough,
legs crossed, on the verge of numb,
eyes tight and close to tears,
all to seek solace in that sacred space
you claim to keep between wake and sleep.

Oh, meta God of Metta,
I paid my fifteen bucks,
to spend this tremulous hour,
in the vicinity of your presence—
but am happy to come this close
to one so full of wonder she believes
there's something more to believe
than how chilly it is down here,
waiting for you, as always,
on the hard gym floor.

New Age Guy

To prolong our time in the ether,
she calls forth a bright light into our midst.
So I unscrunch a little to see the candle
flickering in the middle of the mat
in case it's turned into a burning bush
while I've been gone.
But it remains the same little votive
vying for oxygen in the overheated room.
I fall back to get my share of the air,
the reverie, the peace I've been promised.
But then from deep within,
from a part of me that's long been unacknowledged,
a fart gets loosed that I fear
might frighten our spirit guides
or serve to unnerve my friends
who are not only seeing the light,
but are also, oh God, letting it envelope them,
their darkest fears, fondest hopes,
and those they love and have invited into our circle.

When days later she has us open our eyes,
all smile benignly and claim they did indeed
feel my presence along with them
on our journey.

Sometimes acceptance is the best we can hope,
but much like my time on earth,
I prefer to leave hard evidence
I was actually here.

Plumbing

The Plumber Drops By

Round here, a plumber's 150 bucks an hour and you figure what's been leaking's gotta stop. After an hour or so, I go to the basement to see what's what and he's dead asleep on the cement floor, wrapped in the company parka, my busted pipe a pillow. "Ahem." "Excuse me." Then I drop a bucket on the floor. No movement. Is he dead? I think of yelling, "Flood!" but from the smile on his face, this guy revels in dreams about floods. Finally, I call his boss who says, "Put him on the phone." I say, "How am I gonna do that?" He says, "Don't matter. He ain't much of a talker, anyhow."

The day my plumbing was repaired—

a subway strike. Everyone wheeling to the City, and too early: work, matinees, Christmas blooming. Ken arrived 4 a.m. in his old Elantra, acquired at Korean Rex: bad brakes, bald tires, balky wipers, freezing rain. He, perched on the edge of despair and divorce, and I'd die at his—Hands on the wheel! Asshole—not etherized upon the table. Close, he hit the brakes, slowed to fifteen, and I stumbled into a puddle, discovering life's deepest secret: living's unbearable when your feet are wet. Happy now for a dry gown, ass exposed; happy for dry paper booties; happy for a warm, welcome blanket. Happy of all places, even here.

Grownups

I walk upstairs carrying the laundry
that's been stalled in the basement for days;
this time no one's to blame.
You walk to the family room
where you'll put on but ignore the news.
Later, I'll go out and shift some leaves from side to side
and you'll come to the kitchen and chop some greens.
Once, we'll pass through the same doorway
and, though it might seem awkward for a moment,
we, ourselves, pay no mind to seems.
I will let you go ahead,
out of the habit with which I was raised.
One of us might laugh—

we have lived in this house many years,
have often complained the doorways are too narrow;
the ceilings are of different heights
which have been known to cause
a certain disorientation in some who visit,
and sometimes in those who stay;
the rooms are too small, others would say—
still, we've called this place our home.

There will be a moment later when
I'll head to the john and look in on you
and you won't look up from the paper.
I might even be relieved.
After this—all this—I say to myself
I want to settle somewhere nice
and write a lovely poem,
a poem that sings forgiveness
and the pleasures of arriving at an age.
If you're thinking I won't know how,
you never manage to say.

The Dark

Though I've called the county plenty,
the street light's been out for days
while I've struggled in this moonless winter dark
for the path to the door, crunching
in the now faint footsteps I'd previously made,
and more than once fumbled my keys
and hoped I'd catch them, the way a trapeze artist
might feel for the hands of his mate
in the neon circus dark. But when they fall,
as they will, I pray they'll dent the layer of ice
that's limned the lawn for weeks now,
and might be dug out easy,
and God forbid, not have to hear them
skid down the hill we live atop
and back into the street, which is the direction
I've already come so many times,
and it's dark down there and oh so cold.
Don't buy a house on a hill, the inspector'd said.
You won't be young forever.
Dark magic, that he could tell the future,
and how like me that I was bound,
as if by spell, not to pay him any mind.

System Restore

A feature in Microsoft Windows that allows the user to revert their computer's state ... to that of a previous point in time, which can be used to recover from system malfunctions or other problems.

Given the rate of decay—
memory, word-recall,
such a small percentage
of what we've loved remains
intact, even as we look in the mirror
and examine the lines on the graph that is our face,
or study photos of who we've been
before parts had been removed
and then the body stitched back together
though never again made truly whole.
No wonder we've come to rely
on System Restore to find that one place
from the great and false imagined past
where we can settle in and promise ourselves—
and everyone we've ever loved—
that this time we'll try that much harder
to make everything work.

All That's Known

They spend their time looking forward to the past.

John Osborne

Before

I'm 9 and behind the wheel of our green and white '55 Olds.
I start to check the mirrors,
but my father tells me not to worry
what's coming from behind—though I know he always does.
The Belt curves around to the right near the Bay Parkway exit
and I see houses and parks and empty lots in the distance
and people walking on Shore Road, dressed for the weather.
What's missing is the Verrazano up ahead, that behemoth
that looms over everything on land and on the sea
and whose towers you can hardly ever see in the morning fog.
It's 1958, building it had not yet begun.
Careful, Aloysius, he says to me, though he knows I'm scared
and more apt to wander from my lane unwittingly
than be foolhardy or reckless:
I am my father's son.

This is a game I call *Before*—
and as the bridge appears in the distance today—
as it always does—maybe I can see it new,
an approximation of the wonder that I've lost,
that the years of easy living have worn away.
Imagine seeing it now as if for the first and being stunned
by its grace, its size, its utterness,
the way it swallows up the boats, the streets, the houses,
fathers showing how to sail a boat, to skim a stone;
kids on bikes, their fathers holding on and huffing from behind;
fathers teaching their young how to drive
and secretly pressing an imaginary brake
to slow the car and the press of time;
even a father's memory of all that came before,
and he never got a chance to tell.

Some Day

Who didn't love the el, especially,
the rickety "J" to Brooklyn,
the bus down Metropolitan to Richmond Hill
a Sunday when Dad said he was too tired to drive to Grandpa's,
but really didn't want to go;
me, dressed in my brown plaid suit, yellow shirt,
and climbing the long steel steps to the platform,
the first few easy, then the last, each a longer visit.
Don't let go your sister's hand. My mother was so kindly
but never truly trusted the world, and why would she?
And then waiting for the train—what seemed like forever,
begging to weigh myself and get my fortune—
It's just a penny, Ma!—then, *Why so long? Lemme look.*
Don't you dare get so close to the edge.
And like an old lady told me, smiling, but gently shaking her finger:
The train. You wait, it comes.

Then shimmying on to those wicker seats
and sometimes getting your pants stuck,
the leather straps to hold on, too high for me to reach,
but, *Ma, if I could stand on the seat.*
No, not nice for the others who come after.
but, Someday, I promised myself. Someday.

But some day I would see the photo of those boys
taken, just a few years before I waited so breathless.
Them, staring out from between the slats and barbed wire,
of a train bound to nowhere. Some wailing,
They're bringing us to hell,
others saying, *Everything will be fine. We've been through worse.*
The crying babies, the littler kids asleep in their mothers' arms.
But these boys, just like me,
must've loved the train once—
the screech of steel on steel, the smoke, the halt, the forward feel—
but that, and everything, had drained from their faces
so many stops before the photo was shot.

For Rosh Hashanah

> Victor (Zeke) Zonana (1924–2016)

Now onto this New Year, bad as it promises to be—
there's rumor You, too, have given up,
filled with Your own brand of regret:
seeing us squander our gifts—
wasting our will as if it were a game,
failing to care for our own,
or honor this place we like to call home.
So now You're headed out-of-town,
like some will-o'-the-wisp
to locate some new folks, perhaps, and begin
In the beginning, all over again.

But if I'm wrong and it be Thy will
and You're listening still,
dear God, what the hell,
let us be inscribed again, then sealed.

Though please feel free to pass on him
we've loved so well
who takes his place one final time
and happily chants the ancient prayers
for those of us so far removed, we don't remember how.
But unlike You, our renegade and sometimes vengeful God,
this old man's not rash, nor filled with rage.
But of his own considered will he, too, wants out.
Let it be recorded here, as in Aleppo once,
a temperate man took his life in his hands,
then gently chose—of his own free will—to let it go.

Equinox

Victor (Zeke) Zonana (1924–2016)

Sure is disquieting the way the late summer dark
comes down early and with so little prior notice.
We know the light's been leaving ever since the solstice,
but being human we haven't believed it,
just as we don't believe the old man who's been asleep
on the couch all day won't wake, get on his tennis gear
as always, and head for the court and then cards with his pals.
Till right now when the clouds—gathered red and in layers
looking cave-like in the western sky—we'd gawk like travelers
passing through a strange and lovely land,
and even tried to move toward it,
as if we might find some pyramids below,
perhaps, shutting down for the night, but just in time
to pay homage to the justly famous and ancient dead.

But now we'd rather turn away and to the east
to wait for what we'd always counted on to be inevitable,
and now are not so sure—
break of day and the crossbills and finches
fleeing the blue spruce out front for whatever lies in front of them,
probably the need to survive though we do take great pleasure
mistaking their escape for the joy of being free.
Now the nights will become endless as the days used to be.
Should a lone vesper-sparrow take some time out to sing,
we're done for for sure and will be left forever at a loss.
Who could stand this way at the eastern window
and expect to tolerate such loneliness so long?

My Father Stops at Corners

Jeremiah Walowitz (1916-1987)

The year my father turned 68
he began to cross at corners,
wait for the light, even
for the sign that flashed *Don't Walk*
which he used to ignore and joke,
What if I can't read?
Once they got him for jaywalking
which he did plenty
on Broadway and 28th
where the dress racks whirled
as the cars whizzed too close
and rattled the pint in his pocket
he kept to keep him steady—
but what would he care,
long as he got there quick
and had a story to tell.
He knew he wasn't due to die
till 68, same as his pop,
who some said he looked like,
was built like, barrel-bellied and ruddy
and though he didn't want to hurry it along
saw no need to take chances,
though his heart hurt
and he could hardly breathe
for the terror of living
with his father's death,
which now he owned,
hanging low over his head
like the black fedora
pulled tight over his eyes.

In fact, he made it till 70,
frankly, a little disappointed
at the extra time he had to put in.
And that's what I'm looking at now.
So, please. Don't tell me I look like him,
though I loved that guy
and didn't want to see him
stop at corners—
and when the time was right
I didn't want to see him have to go.

How I Learned

I remember singing songs in that old black jalopy.
My sister and I huddled beneath a blanket—
it was cold those long country drives
and the heat didn't always make it back.
But we had a push-button radio.
Imagine that kind of gadget in a '37 Ford,
one with a running board and klaxon horn.
But my father had had a year,
picked up that baby for a song,
and we were going places.

So we rumbled down that country road,
Lost, my father warned us,
and in that low, portentous voice:
We might never get home.
We shivered at the thought
though knew the consequence
of crying out loud.
And I can hear him now, even as Jack Benny
played "Love in Bloom," telling my mother,
For crying out loud;
the kids can take a joke.
and that's how I learned
we were heading home.

Für Die Kinder

We could never figure out how long
Grandma had been lying on the floor.
She was whimpering my father's name
and we could hear her through the door
when we got home.
That scared the hell out of me—
I already took her for a dybbuk,
as the old ones would say,
the way she suddenly materialized
without a word wherever I happened to be.
My mother explained how her hip must have snapped.
Or she had stumbled in the living room
and it shattered from the fall.
It didn't matter much to me,
except she would soon be gone
from my world on 219th—
first to the hospital, then to the nursing home,
and on to the old people's place, Bat Yam in the Rockaways,
which smelled more like piss than the sea.
And, yes, I would have to visit her there
and still never know what to say.
But at least I wouldn't have to see her warming her hands
over the pilot light as I did my homework
at the kitchen table in the early winter dark.
Or hear her turn down dinner and insist,
Für die Kinder, which smacked of
some other world I wanted nothing of.
Or see her standing at the living room window
late on a summer day,
her mottled face striped by sunlight,
waiting, always waiting,
for my father to come home.

Raking

Starter home? I venture, as I pass the young fellow raking leaves
shed by the maple and oak and red oak, which lined the street
long before any of us arrived.
Could be a finisher, he laughs—we've practiced this before—
as maybe he considers how he's gonna pay for this tiny Cape
plunked down in what the realtor convinced him
was the best school district on the North Shore.
Then I remark, my way back, nursing an old man's coffee—
the 99 cent Special from the Mobil On-the-Go,
bitter, black, and tall to last all day—
as he wrestles leaves into a black plastic bag
that's sure to decompose in some far-off future
even his son, who's playing in the leaves, will never see.
Back in the day, we used to burn 'em, I say.
Huh? he replies, as if this were also a joke
he might have heard before, and he takes a few off the stack,
steals a look left, then right, then left,
for the imagined environmental cops or volunteer fire brigade
out to raise money for their fancy new truck.
Then from his pocket he takes a Bic—
and lights an oak leaf, then a maple, then another still
till he has in hand a long-lost autumn fire.
The wind's blowing my way and I breathe
a bit of my childhood that some days I try to forget.

Smells good, I say, not wanting to let on the places
I've just been taken, the fires up and down the streets,
the crackle of leaves still a little wet,
the men, just back from the war,
some somber, some sober, some trying to be,
tending the home-fires now and wondering
what it had all been about, the loss, the hope,
the generation growing inside already tending
the slow-burning fires of mistrust and resentment
and hardly anyone venturing a reason why.

Button Trends—Summer, 1959

I was 10 and ready for work:
lunch order in my fist, a ten in one pocket
mail stuffed in the other—
But never down the mail chute,
my father said as I headed to the elevator,
something might get stuck
and there goes the business,—though business
was never much up on 8, at 1181 Bway,
and I used to hear him on the phone
—*Doll, doncha know the check is in the mail,*—
with that confidential laugh that got him so far, no farther.
You got to take the mail and get it right in the box;
Aloysius, this ain't horseshoes. Though Hubert,
the black delivery boy who had signed on
to learn this dying business,
would mumble *Horseshit* in its place,
though I wasn't supposed to hear.
So I'd head out on the street,
to listen to the Jamaican guy
who hunkered near the entrance
banging away on his homemade pan;
and the old Jews—Commies, anarchists,
artists-schmartists—as they made their way
toward Parnes Dairy across the street,
always in the middle of some tzimmis
and now ready to kvetch about the size of the dollop
that came in their borscht.

And the old Irish jocks, no place to go,
Belmont closed for repairs, Jamaica shut for good,
and how the hell d'ya get to Aqueduct anyhow.
And in all that whirl to find my way back to 28th St.
seemed like plenty to do,
turned around and dizzy among the dress racks,
carrying two corned beef, one pastrami, one tongue,
a cream, ginger ale, and Celray to share,
sides of slaw, packed in cardboard, and leaking through the bag.
Except when the elevator got back to 8,
I still had the envelopes in my pocket
and had to drop them down the chute—
the checks never to arrive, the invoices not to be paid,
statements of accounts ignored, bills of lading denied,
the aroma never to be delivered, but all over the mail.

My Father's Cake

If I wanted cake, I would've ordered one,
he manages from the darkness of the hall,
a joke, even at this late hour.
He tumbles into a chair and inspects the scene—
us, our gifts, and what my mother's baked,
the candles already lit—the readiness is all—
then nods weak thanks as if
we were strangers come to his house
and soon his slow rising is to show us the door
and bid a polite goodbye.
But he pauses just past mid-arc, his face
a sad balloon bobbing helpless
above the cake, and when he finds
some breath to take, his wrinkles fade
and he becomes a cartoon-father:
red, distorted, and about to explode.
And as he does, he blows the candles out
one for this birthday, one for the next,
expelling the long, tired breaths
so they deflect clear across the table
and air becomes flame, smoke, and finally
my mother's smile. You see, she seems to say.
You see. Then as final curtain, all sing
as father performs the old disappearance,
his footsteps growing faint as the sounds
of the world when we're weary and diving
straight toward sleep. My mother sighs and says,
*You know, he's never been sick
a day in his life.* Only when we nod
does she begin to cut the cake. How expertly
she clears the knife, moving it
in and out a glass of water.

A Cottage in Sag Harbor

My mother showed me the photo,
the cottage, the sea, the shore
and told me we needed to go—
away from here, and him,
and everything that was going wrong.
It would be best for us all
and, she swore, it would be just a while,
maybe two weeks, a month, or the whole summer
if we liked. I could call it a vacation,
if my friends should ask, though I knew they would know.
And it's nice out there and cool with a breeze
and we'd take a bus and bring only what we need.
My kid brother would thrive in the sun, the sand—
and even if not, we'd have each other,
and Dad will be fine,
he knows how to care for himself—
he can open a can of soup and make eggs.
I looked at my father, dead asleep
on the floor, and told her—
till then, the hardest thing I'd ever said—
Looks nice, Mom,
but I think I'm staying here with him.

Half-Life

Small change always burned a hole in my pocket:
had just enough to eat, or to smoke,
or could blow it all on pinball in the lounge—
had to find something to do with these hands,
restless from loneliness with hours to kill before my next class—
studying useless as usual, the library a morgue
with nothing to do but turn pages
and steal looks at the studious girls
I pretended I didn't want. Though in the library lobby
I found one free spirit who read palms for free,
as close as I'd get to hold anyone's hand
for quite some time. *Your love line is jagged*, she told me
not confidentially—she liked the audience that had gathered.
You'll be married many times, and each will end unhappy.
My face must've fallen as I realized she, who held onto my wrist
more like a vise than a soft word,
would be another I'd never have,
given the odds against our long-term happiness.
And then she amended some comfort: *No need to worry;
I see by your lifeline you're bound to die young—*
this a sure sign I should buy a pack of smokes,
skip Physics again, and contemplate the half-life,
which I happened to be already living—
and whatever of it might still be to come.

Downsizing

No tears when the stately old divan
departed. Only when the new owner
sawed off its middle leg to get through
the door, did it give my mother pause.
Meanwhile her three remaining pals
dutifully chose one shmata each
they'll surely never wear themselves,
but come Christmas might offer the help.
Finally, a few items had to be trashed
—moldy *Good Housekeepings*: recipes
she couldn't bear to part with,
but never good enough to make;
tchotchkes varie: the alligator nut-cracker
from the Everglades, Baby Big Ben
that once played *God Save the Queen*,
olive oil we pressed ourselves in Spain,
surely rancid now,—then we thought we were done.
Till we looked at the glacier
that had formed in the freezer:
Interred there like a twelfth century mountaineer
hiding lost truths, were meals from lifetimes ago:
a meatloaf from the 90s buried behind
more recent triumphs; half pints of milk
smuggled from the Senior Center in case of natural disaster.
And this, a shriveled piece of wedding cake.
Ma, that was to be eaten
your first anniversary, for luck.
She pauses, thinks about her husband
long dead, longer mourned and says,
Maybe that's why things didn't work out—
and drops it in the trash.

The Cost of Bread

I'd come home from school some days
to find Harold Dugan from the bakery truck
taking a spin on my mother's old calculator.
Or for all I knew on my mother—
an old rumor that hardly matters now.
But she sure knew how to make his numbers work
as they spun out on those rolls of tape
and, times being tough, how to defray the cost of bread.
And he was a smooth talker, that Harold,
and school wasn't done till three
and he owned his route
and he made his own time.

My mother kept books her whole life—
in her head and with a careful hand—
but now the numbers spin all over the page
and she can't pin them down.
When the doctor asks her to draw a clock,
it looks like a scrambled egg,
the numbers floating in and out of the shell.
Draw three o'clock, the doctor orders,
and she says it's too early for lunch.
I tell her, *Ma, we already ate*
and my mother informs me—and for my own good—
she can eat any time she damn well pleases.

Remembering Ralph Edwards

My mother, a practical sort, never offered
the forced élan of long-term wanting,
or the thrill of spontaneous combustion.
In fact, she never made demands at all—
till now, when she announces to any who'll listen:
I want my personality back.

I don't know where to go to get,
but I've learned how to distract—
to talk about the weather;
how the kids are doing in school;
how you have to sleep the night
if you want to keep whatever world you've got
from bursting into flame.
That's nothing, she hisses, like a long, slow leak,
then waves her arms, elbows locked,
as if they're meant to break like waves,
as if that would show me how.

This is the stuff you never got
at your mother's apron strings
as you learned to pair the socks,
counted pennies into rolls,
or yelled *Rummy* loud enough
to be heard in a roomful of Jews.
If I had the guts I'd exclaim,
Esther, this is your life!
Then my practical mother
might return for just a moment and add,
Whether you asked for it or not,
or even better, maybe she'd say,
Not now, I'm busy.

All That's Known

My mother fallen, hip cracked, now replaced,
sits slumped in the hospital chair,
where the nurse and aide have plunked her
like a half-filled bag of laundry
no one's hurrying to reach and make clean.
She seems to wait for nothing
and not to be able to say,
she who would talk to the wall I was
till she was blue in the face.
But what's unsaid makes a life—
and this late hour I'm finally ready to hear:
Tears instead, despite her effort to stanch them,
she who once proclaimed the ice water in those veins,
and though the color's drained from her glacier-face
what flows away is proof
that everything I've heard her say
about herself is wrong.
All that's known of anyone is tiny,
an iceberg perched and dancing on the sea,
compared to what sits brooding far below
secret and unfathomable.

Offerings for the Dead

Second thoughts sometimes detract
from who you figured you might be
in the distillery of your dreams—
you'd help those in need, comfort the afflicted,
mourn the dead, or at least offer compassion
to those who had been much closer
and in words they could easily take in at a time like this.
A sincere "I don't know what to say" often turns out
to be better receiving-line chatter
than "My condolences, Ma'am, though
I don't have the faintest notion who you are."
Such expressions are often distracting,
and you end up in a handshake that knows no end,
or, God forbid, you hug a stranger
for much too long, and in this dance you have nothing more to say,
and instead begin to babble tidbits from the past—
memories that might just as well be inventions—
and before long you're blubbering when
all you wanted was a little silent weeping in a corner,
far from the sight of the deceased, who you really liked,
your voice cracking at the seams and anything
real you were planning to say jumbled and fumfered
like your own worst vision of yourself,
a kid whose mother dragged him to a wake—
where he might at least have learned something useful
for later in life when his mother is gone.

My History in Valhalla

I once fell for a woman who liked to say:
There are no accidents—
Her way of assuring me
I'd live and be well
without waiting around
for her to stumble into my arms.

But now the governor, surely wise,
— and of a practical bent—
assures the public:
Sometimes there will be accidents at railroad crossings,
and with them will come death and great loss.
Hence, we need no wasteful speculation.

But sometimes life just hands us such purposelessness
even in a place named Valhalla,—
what ought to be this little slice of heaven,
but with schools and hospitals, cemeteries and railroad crossings,
so many signals we should have heeded of impending misery,
and of gods meddling willy-nilly in men's affairs.

This was the same Valhalla where,
when I was a kid, I was sure
I killed a bunch of strangers in a car, quite by accident,
at the very moment I learned I was in love—
and my life would be over,
just as it was readying to start.

Then the other day, it was here in Valhalla
I picked up a shovel,
dug into the mountain of cold winter dirt, assembled
with such care, to bury a friend: this, a kindness, I was assured.
O, praise be a life that can bear the weight
of one sad intention after another.

Coda

*Every moment happens twice: inside and outside,
and they are two different histories.*

Zadie Smith

The Story of "The Story of the Milkman"

Nicole (Lucivero) Martini never met her grandfather Nick for whom she's named. Her brother Nicholas never met him either. Their father, also Nicholas Lucivero, never met his father, Nick, who had died six months before he was born. Her cousin, Anthony Maraglino, never met his grandfather, Nick Lucivero either.

Rose Esposito, Nick Lucivero's sister remembers her brother as a war hero who landed on Normandy Beach in June 1944, a great athlete, a guy who lit up a room when he walked in. She's told all her family's young the stories about her brother, Nick, who died more than sixty years ago on January 30, 1957, in a tragic accident at the Locust Manor Station near Farmers and Baisley Blvd in St. Albans, when his milk delivery truck was hit by a Long Beach-bound Long Island Rail Road train. The watchman had fallen asleep in the early morning hours and failed to lower the gate to stop the oncoming milk truck driven by Nick Lucivero. Accompanying him was his assistant Courtney Kimble, who was 17 and just about to graduate from high school.

I was in third grade, not quite 8 years old the morning this happened—and Nick Lucivero was my milkman. For all I know, he might have been on his way to deliver milk to my house in Cambria Heights, a little more than two and a half miles away. I might have met Nick once or twice, though I can't say for sure. After all, milkmen were denizens of a nocturnal world a kid wouldn't know much about. But hearing about the death of our milkman shook my world. Kids in middle class Cambria Heights were pretty sheltered in our neighborhood with neat lawns and sturdy houses on tree-lined blocks. Our fathers had fought in the war and didn't like to talk about it much. Our mothers mostly didn't work outside the home and were there when we walked home for lunch, and at 3 o'clock when school let out. Things went wrong, of course, but nothing had ever happened as tragically and unexpectedly as this, and never so close to home. Yeah, I was an overprotected, sensitive kid who was disproportionally affected by such things; I spent a lot of time living inside my own head; I even grew up to be a poet. But the story of the death of the milkman haunted me and has stayed with me my whole life, enough so that I wrote a poem about the event. The poem is called "The Story of the Milkman" and Melanie Villines, the publisher of Silver Birch Press, was kind enough to publish it on her website in 2015.

A year and a half later, Anthony Maraglino was conducting some internet research on his family and hoped to find more information about his larger-than-life grandfather who he'd only heard about and never met. In the course of that research, he found a reference to a poem called "The Story of the Milkman." He traced it to the Silver Birch Press website and found the poem I had written. Along with the poem, I included a paragraph which told the "true" story of Nick Lucivero, at least as true as far as I could piece it together. Anthony passed the poem on to his family, including his cousin Nicole and his

Aunt Rosie. Anthony also found me on Facebook and sent me a message telling me of his connection to the poem and how reading it had moved him. Shortly after, I was notified by Melanie Villines, the publisher of Silver Birch, that there was a new comment posted about "The Story of the Milkman," this one written by the milkman's sister Rose Esposito, now in her 80s and who'd experienced this tragedy first-hand, and who remembered her brother lovingly.

Then, I was contacted by Stephen Blackburne, a friend of Nicole (Lucivero) Martini. Stephen had purchased a copy of my book, *Exactly Like Love* (Osedax Press, 2016) in which the poem also appears. He asked me to autograph the book, so he could give it to Nicole as a gift. Soon, I heard directly from Nicole, who told me how much reading the poem and having a copy of the book meant to her. In her email, she wrote, "Thank you also for writing your poem—my father, who will be 60 in June, never met his father. The accident occurred six months before he was born. This poem has given us all reason to talk about my grandfather and has, in just a few short weeks, allowed my father to come to terms with things he hasn't thought about in forty-plus years."

I can't know exactly what Nicole means, but I do know this: Most regular folks—and good folks they are, too—don't much care for poetry. Marianne Moore confessed in her famous poem "Poetry" that she too dislikes it. When pressed, people often say they don't understand it. They usually blame a high school English teacher and, as a retired high school English teacher myself, I'll even accept some of the blame. Others like to quote the poet WH Auden who said, "Poetry makes nothing happen," perhaps a way to explain their preference for an editorial that angers them, for a touching and well-written obituary, or a good love story. But "The Story of the Milkman," my poem, actually made something happen. Perhaps it's not a big thing, unless you consider connecting with some strangers, and helping them connect with their own pasts over the distance of nearly sixty years to be something. I think it is.

Acknowledgments

My thanks to the following editors of journals, anthologies, and chapbooks where these works have previously appeared:

A-3 Review: In Favor of Forgetting (Winner, A-3 Review Contest, May, 2017)

Ain't Got No Press, A Poet's Siddur: Lehkah Dodi

Autumn Sky Poetry Daily: The Cost of Bread, Tremont, All That's Known, Downsizing, Moving Day (Pushcart Prize Nominee), Photo of Snow in the Suburbs, A Cottage in Sag Harbor

Border Line Press, In Transit: Brooklyn Bound

*Borders and Boundaries, Blue Thread Book*s*:* Remembering Ralph Edwards (Finalist, Alexander and Dora Raynes Poetry Competition, 2017)

The Drabble: The day my plumbing was repaired

The Ekphrastic Review: January the Tenth

Facts, Fakes, and Fictions, Blue Thread Books: Home of the Sages (Finalist, Alexander and Dora Raynes Poetry Competition, 2018)

Hobart: The Infield Fly Rule

Jewish Literary Journal: Für Die Kinder, Divorce

Leannan: Here, Marriage Song

Local Gems Press, Recession, Depression and Economic Reflection: Sunrise Fire

Medusa's Laugh Press, Lost: Reflections: How I Learned

Medusa's Laugh Press, Microtext Anthology 4: The Plumber Drops By

Melancholy Hyperbole: My History in Valhalla, Out for a Drive and Thinking about John Ferone, No Heat, Before

The Moon Magazine: A Kind Breeze

Muddy River Poetry Review: The Dark (also appeared in *Autumn Sky Poetry Daily*)

Napalm and Novocain: Endings Set Us Free

Newtown Literary: Waiting for the Singularity

The New Verse News: Guys like us, Christmas Past with the Trumps, Don't Get Sick in America, Lordy, I Hope There Are Tapes, For Rosh Hashanah, Role Models, Revision (Pushcart Prize Nominee, 2018)

Osedax Press, Beneficial Exercises for Heart Disturbances: A Dry Well

Perfume River Poetry Review: Video Postcard from Vietnam

Poetry Super Highway, Yom HaShoah Poetry Issue: Some Day

Postcard Poems and Prose: Coming Soon, Last Dream of Morning

Pure Slush Books, Tall...ish: Tony's Wake

Pure Slush (online): My Father's Cake

Queens Times-Ledger: The Story of The Story of the Milkman, orginally published as Death of milkman on train tracks haunts poet's memories of his youth

Red Wolf Journal: The Sequel, You Are Home, Hailstorm, Offerings for the Dead

Sheila-Na-Gig: System Restore, Grownups, Stress Test, My Father Stops at Corners

Silver Birch Press: Button Trends—Summer 1959, The Story of the Milkman, Half-Life

Verse-Virtual: My mother wears a mask for Mardi Gras, 1938 Philco 4XX (also appeared in *The Ekphrastic Review*), The Golf Poem, Metta Prayer, Equinox, Poem-a-Night, Anthony Peter Tumbarello, Poem for the End of Daylight Savings, Motion is medicine, you tell me (also appeared in *Autumn Sky Poetry Daily*), String Theory, Waiting for Flowers, In the Company of English Teachers, Raking, Roadkill

The following poems were published in my chapbook, *Exactly Like Love*, published by *Osedax Press*, 2016: The Story of the Milkman, A Dry Well, Here, Für Die Kinder, My History in Valhalla, Grace

Thanks

In addition to the editors of the publications listed on the preceding pages—those who have presented my work prior to the publication of *The Story of the Milkman and Other Poems*—a special thank you goes to:

Firestone Feinberg, editor and publisher of Verse-Virtual: A Community Journal of Poetry. Each month, Firestone allows my work to see the light of day online, even when the value of that work sometimes eludes him; frankly, it sometimes also eludes me. However, that kind of faith is rare in a publisher.

Morgan Adams, publisher of Osedax Press, who shepherded my chapbook *Exactly Like Love* from manuscript into print. Morgan is a fine and thoughtful editor, and she helped create and design a memorable chapbook, even if the poems inside it weren't always so memorable.

Matt Potter, publisher and editor of the Bequem Publishing collective, which includes the Truth Serum imprint. Matt is tireless and committed to publishing voices that are sometimes not heard in the corporate publishing world. Despite the flaws in the poems within, Matt makes it his business that all the books that bear his imprints are handsome and very well-made.

Melanie Villines, editor and publisher of the late, and lamented, Silver Birch Press, who first published the poem, *The Story of the Milkman*.

Roz Liston, editor of the Queens Times-Ledger News, for publishing the original version of *The Story of "The Story of the Milkman"* as *Death of milkman on train tracks haunts poet's memories of his youth*.

And to Corey Kilgannon of the New York Times, who found that story in the Queens Times-Ledger News and from it wrote his story, *Ode to a Milkman, Killed 60 Years Ago, Soothes His Family*, which appeared in the New York Times on April 16, 2017.

My wife, Jeanette Walowitz—who took the beautiful photo which graces the cover of this book—and my daughter, Jamie Walowitz, both of whom allowed me to fret over these poems, sometimes to the point of distraction or obsession. Their love and patience for me is legendary—and seemingly boundless.

My sister, Helene Berger and my brother, David Walowitz, who've never complained as I've told and re-told, transformed, and even disfigured, as writers often do, stories about my parents, Jerry and Esther Walowitz, to whom this book is dedicated. I wish that they were alive to see the publication of this book—and to tell me, only half-kidding, to stop lying about them.

My friends, some of whom are brilliant and inspiring poets who I learn from regularly. Still others have expressed little interest in poetry, but have humored me and have sometimes listened when I've spoken to them about the way I spend my time. Some of them have even admitted to liking one or two of my poems.

About the Author

Alan Walowitz has been writing poetry, sometimes successfully and sometimes un-, for more than 50 years. He has a small portion of an MFA in Writing from Goddard College, and has an entire degree from Eastern Connecticut State University and several from Queens College of the City University of NY. He's studied with poets Estha Weiner, Fred Marchant, C.K. Williams, Carol Muske, Colette Inez, and Stephen Stepanchev, among others who probably would not want their names mentioned with his.

Though writing poems can be quite lucrative, Alan has earned the bulk of his fortune as a teacher and supervisor of secondary English for 34 years. His poems can be found lots of places on the web and off. He's a Contributing Editor at *Verse-Virtual*, an Online Community Journal of Poetry, and teaches at Manhattanville College in Purchase, New York.

The poem "The Story of the Milkman" was featured in an article in *The New York Times* on April 16, 2017: https://www.nytimes.com/2017/04/16/nyregion/ode-to-a-milkman-killed-60-years-ago-soothes-his-family.html.

Alan's chapbook, *Exactly Like Love*, is in its second printing and is available from Osedax Press.

Visit Alan's website at http://alanwalowitz.com/.

Also from TRUTH SERUM PRESS

https://truthserumpress.net/catalogue/

- *Minotaur and Other Stories* by Salvatore Difalco
  978-1-925536-79-9 (paperback) 978-1-925536-80-5 (eBook)
- *The Book of Acrostics* by John Lambremont, Sr.
  978-1-925536-52-2 (paperback) 978-1-925536-53-9 (eBook)
- *Square Pegs* by Rob Walker
  978-1-925536-62-1 (paperback) 978-1-925536-63-8 (eBook)

  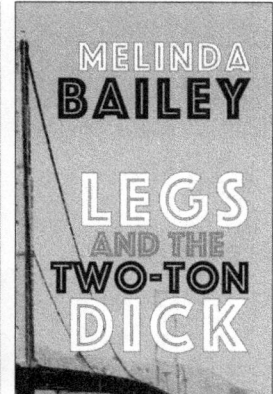

- *Cheat Sheets* by Edward O'Dwyer
  978-1-925536-60-7 (paperback) 978-1-925536-61-4 (eBook)
- *The Crazed Wind* by Nod Ghosh
  978-1-925536-58-4 (paperback) 978-1-925536-59-1 (eBook)
- *Legs and the Two-Ton Dick* by Melinda Bailey
  978-1-925536-37-9 (paperback) 978-1-925536-38-6 (eBook)

Also from TRUTH SERUM PRESS

https://truthserumpress.net/catalogue/

- *Dollhouse Masquerade* by Samuel E. Cole
  978-1-925536-43-0 (paperback) 978-1-925536-44-7 (eBook)
- *Kiss Kiss* by Paul Beckman
  978-1-925536-21-8 (paperback) 978-1-925536-22-5 (eBook)
- *Inklings* by Irene Buckler
  978-1-925536-41-6 (paperback) 978-1-925536-42-3 (eBook)

- *On the Bitch* by Matt Potter
  978-1-925536-45-4 (paperback) 978-1-925536-46-1 (eBook)
- *Too Much of the Wrong Thing* by Claire Hopple
  978-1-925536-33-1 (paperback) 978-1-925536-34-8 (eBook)
- *Track Tales* by Mercedes Webb-Pullman
  978-1-925536-35-5 (paperback) 978-1-925536-36-2 (eBook)

Also from TRUTH SERUM PRESS

https://truthserumpress.net/catalogue/

- *Luck and Other Truths* by Richard Mark Glover
  978-1-925101-77-5 (paperback) 978-1-925536-04-1 (eBook)
- *Hello Berlin!* by Jason S. Andrews
  978-1-925536-11-9 (paperback) 978-1-925536-12-6 (eBook)
- *Deer Michigan* by Jack C. Buck
  978-1-925536-25-6 (paperback) 978-1-925536-26-3 (eBook)

  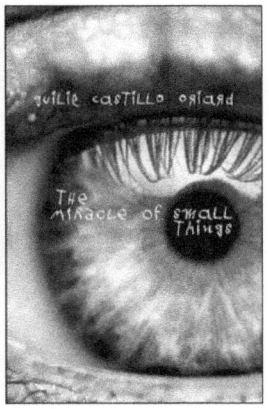

- *What Came Before* by Gay Degani
  978-1-925536-05-8 (paperback) 978-1-925536-06-5 (eBook)
- *Rain Check* by Levi Andrew Noe
  978-1-925536-09-6 (paperback) 978-1-925536-10-2 (eBook)
- *The Miracle of Small Things* by Guilie Castillo Oriard
  978-1-925101-73-7 (paperback) 978-1-925101-74-4 (eBook)

www.ingramcontent.com/pod-product-compliance
Lightning Source LLC
Chambersburg PA
CBHW051808040426
42446CB00007B/576